ABOUT THE BOOK

One of the most popular of all American sports, football is played by elementary school, high school, college, and professional teams. Millions of people crowd football stadiums or watch games on television.

Here is a book for young readers who want to know all about the game— how it is played, the various playing positions, basic offensive and defensive strategy. There is a bit of football history, a close-up look at the field and equipment, and an explanation of competition at the different levels, with various conferences, leagues, and ruling bodies defined.

All-time favorite players (as determined by a New York Times/CBS poll), including Joe Namath, O.J. Simpson, Roger Staubach and Jim Brown, are profiled. Statistics list all-time records. A glossary of football terms is included.

GEORGE SULLIVAN *is a free-lance writer known for his sports books. He is the author of over 100 non-fiction titles.*

Mr. Sullivan writes for both adults and young readers and, in response to requests from librarians, he prepared All About Football, a volume on football basics and highlights at the fourth grade reading level. Now he offers the game of baseball in a similar presentation.

George Sullivan was born in Lowell, Massachusetts, and was graduated from Fordham University. He lives in New York City.

ALL ABOUT
FOOTBALL

George Sullivan

Illustrated with photographs and diagrams

G. P. PUTNAM'S SONS　　　　　　　　　　　*New York*

Frontispiece: Running back Allen Pinkett of the University of Notre Dame gallops for yardage against Colorado.

PICTURE CREDITS

CBS-TV, 85, 95; Chicago Bears, 114; New York Public Library, 64; Pro Football Hall of Fame, 73, 76; San Francisco 49ers, 30; University of Nebraska, 70; University of Notre Dame, Steven Navratil, 2. All other photographs are by George Sullivan.

Published in 1990 by G. P. Putnam's Sons,
a division of The Putnam & Grosset Group,
200 Madison Avenue, New York, NY 10016.
Originally published in 1987 by Dodd, Mead & Co., Inc.
Published simultaneously in Canada.
Printed in the United States of America.
Book design by Jean Krulis.

Library of Congress Cataloging-in-Publication Data
Sullivan, George, date–
All about football / George Sullivan. p. cm.
Reprint. Originally published: New York:
Dodd, Mead. © 1987. Includes index.
SUMMARY: Explains the game of football, presenting
its history and profiles of leading players. 1. Football—
Juvenile literature. [1. Football.] I. Title. [GV950.7S87
1990] 796.332'2—dc19 88-34081 CIP AC
ISBN 0-399-61227-0 (hardcover)
3 5 7 9 10 8 6 4 2
ISBN 0-399-21907-2 (paperback)
1 3 5 7 9 10 8 6 4 2

FIRST PAPERBACK IMPRESSION

The author is grateful to the many people who con-
tributed information and photographs for use in this
book. Special thanks are due: Don Smith, Pro Football
Hall of Fame; Ed Croke, Director of Media Services,
New York Giants; Jim Greenidge, Director of Public-
ity, New England Patriots; Mike Gigante, National
Football League, Francesca Kurti, TLC Custom Labs;
John Devaney and Aime LaMontagne.

CONTENTS

INTRODUCTION

Football, a rough sport that grew out of two kicking games, soccer and rugby, is an American favorite.

The game is played in elementary schools and high schools. It is played by colleges and the professional teams of the National Football League, the NFL.

While it is popular as a sport to play, it is even more popular as a sport to watch. Football is, in fact, the most-watched of all American sports. Millions of fans crowd stadiums to watch their favorite teams. Many millions of others follow the sport on television.

Football and television grew up together during the 1950s. The two go together like cool drinks on a hot day. Popular football teams, such as the Dallas Cowboys or Miami Dolphins, are popular in the same way "The Cosby Show" is popular. Year in and year out, the Super Bowl, the game that decides the pro football championship, is one of the highest rated of all TV shows. Around 100 million people watch it.

Why is football so popular on television?

It's partly because football is not an easy sport to watch. Television helps us to understand what's happening on the field.

Watching at a stadium, you can get confused. On a given signal, twenty-two players, almost all of them motionless, suddenly spring into action. It's hard to know what's going on.

Many plays seem to end in meaningless pileups. The groups of players streaming on and off the field add to the confusion.

But television, with its split-screen images and instant replay, helps you to understand each play. And there are commentators to explain things.

This book will also help. It examines football's most important rules. It surveys the game's strategy and tactics. There's a close-up look at some of the game's best-liked players. There's some football history.

You'll get a lot more out of watching football after reading this book. You'll be able to look at the game with an expert's eye.

1

SOME BASICS

Football is played by two teams of eleven players each. The idea of the game is for one team to move the football across the opposition's goal line at one end of the field. This results in a touchdown. A touchdown is worth six points.

If the team is unable to cross the opponent's goal line and score a touchdown, the team at least tries to move the ball close enough to the opposition goalposts to kick the ball over the crossbar and between the two uprights. This is a field goal. It is worth three points.

These and some of the game's other fundamentals are explained in this chapter.

The Field

Football's playing field is a rectangle. It is 120 yards long and 53⅓ yards wide. The field's surface may be

11

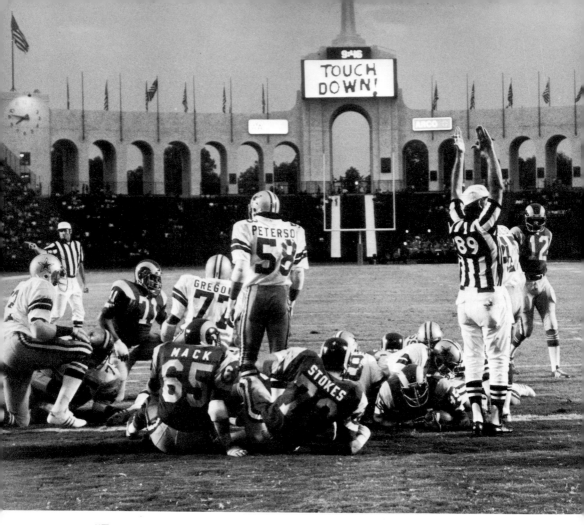

"Touchdown" signals the official, and the scoreboard agrees.

natural grass or a green synthetic surface, such as AstroTurf.

Near each end of the field is a goal line. The distance between the two lines is 100 yards. Extending beyond each goal line is an end zone that is 10 yards deep.

The goalposts, through which the ball can be kicked,

are on the goal line in high school and college football. They are on the end line, that is, at the end of the 10-yard end zone, in professional football.

The two goalpost uprights, are connected by a crossbar. The crossbar is 10 feet above the ground.

In professional football, the uprights are 18½ feet apart. High school and college kickers have a larger (and closer) target. The uprights for them are 23 feet, 4 inches apart.

The field is marked with white lines every five yards. A sideline borders each long side of the field. Any player who touches or crosses a sideline is ruled out of bounds.

Midfield is the 50-yard line. From there, the yard lines are described in terms of the defending team. For instance, Denver's 28-yard line is 28 yards up the field from the goal that Denver is defending. Denver is also 72 yards from the opposition's goal line. (While the yard lines are five yards apart, the in-between lines are marked by short lines at the sidelines or at the middle of the field, or both.)

Two other sets of lines are important. These are the hash marks.

The two sets of hash marks extend from goal line to goal line near the center of the field. A play begins with the ball on the hash marks. Suppose on that play the ballcarrier goes out of bounds. An official then takes the ball and places it on the nearest hash mark

HIGH SCHOOL AND COLLEGE
FIELD OF PLAY

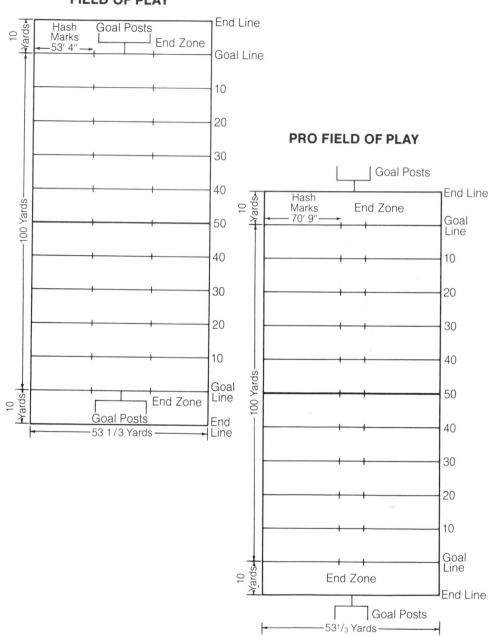

Hash marks and yard lines help out performers in lining up for a half-time show.

for the next play. This also happens whenever a play ends in the area between the hash marks and the sideline.

In professional football, the hash marks are 70 feet, 9 inches from each sideline. In high school and college play, they're 53 feet, 4 inches from each sideline.

The Ball

The oval football is approximately 11 inches long and about 7 inches in diameter at its center. It weighs

Official football is 11 inches long, weighs 14 to 15 ounces.

from 14 to 15 ounces. It is inflated to an air pressure of 12½ to 13½ pounds per square inch.

Scoring

This is the way points are scored:
- 6 points for a touchdown (carrying or passing the ball across the opposition goal line).
- 3 points for a field goal (kicking the ball over the crossbar and through the goalposts).
- 2 points for a safety (forcing the other team to down the ball behind its own goal line).
- 1 point for the extra point allowed after scoring a touchdown. (A pro team can kick, run, or pass for

the extra point from the 2-yard line. College and high school rules give two points if the points are made by a run or a pass, one point if by a kick. When the ball is kicked, it is placed on the 3-yard line).

Players' Equipment

Players wear jerseys and pants that fit snugly. This makes it difficult for opposition players to grasp a player's clothing when trying to tackle.

Players wear shoes with cleats of hard rubber or plastic. The cleats screw into the shoe bottom. Cleats are often cone-shaped but their size and shape varies according to the surface on which the game is being played. Cleats used on grass are a different shape than those used on artificial surfaces.

On artificial turf, players often wear cleats that look like this.

Each player wears a shell-plastic helmet that is held in place with a chin guard. The helmet is fitted with a facemask. The facemask varies in size according to the player's position. A lineman's helmet, for instance, has a facemask that protects him from his eyebrows to his chin. A quarterback, who has to be able to see the entire field clearly, may have only a slim, clear plastic bar to protect the lower part of his face.

Each player wears a mouthpiece to help prevent injuries to his teeth.

Players wear many different types of pads under their uniforms. They all wear shoulder pads, hip pads, thigh pads, and knee pads. The thigh pads and knee pads slip into special pockets sewn into the pants. Elbow pads and rib pads are also common.

Canadian Football

Football is popular is only one other country of the world besides the United States, and that's Canada. The game is played in high schools in Canada, by some two dozen Canadian colleges and universities, and by the nine professional teams that make up the Canadian Football League.

Tackle Howard Richards of the Dallas Cowboys peers out from behind his facemask.

Quarterback Joe Theismann, who starred for the Washington Redskins during late 1970s and early 1980s, began his pro career with the Toronto Argonauts of the Canadian Football League.

However, Canadian and American football are not quite the same. The Canadian field is bigger, for one thing. It's 110 yards long and 65 yards wide, and there are two 25-yard end zones.

And, in Canada, there are twelve players on a side. The added man, called a backfielder, usually lines up in the backfield but, when being used as a pass receiver, he can line up as an end. On defense, the twelfth man usually serves as a deep defensive back.

Scoring is different, too. On the Canadian field, the two lines at the end of the field (known as end lines in American football) are called deadlines. On a kickoff or a punt, the receiving team must advance the ball out of the area between the deadline and the goal line. If the receiving team fails to do this, the kicking team gets a point. This point is called a single, or rouge.

Many observers say that Canadian football is more exciting than American football. Since the field is bigger, there's more of an emphasis on speed and agility. Sometimes outstanding American college players, considered too light for NFL play, become stars in the Canadian Football League.

OFFENSE vs. DEFENSE

A typical pro football game has about five touchdowns, a couple of field goals, some 120 or 130 plays, and takes approximately three hours.

During that time, the possession of the ball is constantly shifting back and forth from one team to the other. The team with the ball, that is, the team trying to score points, is called the offensive team. The team trying to prevent points is the defensive team.

As one team tries to score points, and the other tries to prevent scoring, players are allowed to block and tackle—hit each other. And they're allowed to hit hard. In fact, the team that hits the hardest is usually the team that wins.

As this suggests, football is a violent game. You can tell that from the players' nicknames. There's The Hammer and The Assassin, and the Pittsburgh Steelers once had a player named *Mean* Joe Greene.

Football is not a gentle game. Here University of Pennsylvania tacklers upend a Bucknell ballcarrier.

The Offensive Team

The offensive team is made up of seven linemen and four backs.

The man at the center of the line is called the center. It is his job to snap the ball back between his legs to the quarterback to begin play. Or he may pass the ball back between his legs to a punter or to the

Scoreboard urges home team—the Giants—to wage war on the opposition.

man assigned to hold the ball on place-kicks. The center also must block.

The linemen on either side of the center were once supposed to guard the center as he snapped the ball back. For that reason, they were called guards. Their job now is to block—but they're still called guards.

The two men who line up just outside the guards

are blockers, too. They're called tackles (although they're not allowed to do any tackling. At one time, they were permitted to tackle, however.)

These five players—the center, two guards, and two tackles—are called the interior linemen. The two men at the end of the line are called ends. Like the other members of the offensive line, the ends do some blocking but their chief job is to catch passes.

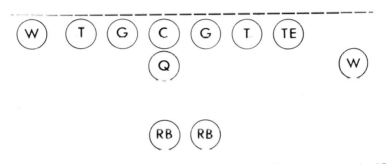

The offensive team is made up of a center (C), two guards (G), two tackles (T), a tight end (TE), two wide receivers (W), a quarterback (Q), and two running backs (RB).

Ends often have special names. In pro football, the end on the right side of the line lines up close to the tackle and is called the tight end. On most plays, his job is to block but he is also very important as a pass receiver.

Pro teams position the end on the other side of the line several yards from the tackle. He is called a wide receiver. In college play, this end is called a split

Quarterback handles the ball on almost every play.

end. Whatever term is used, this end's main job is to catch passes.

So much for the offensive line. Now the backfield.

The back who lines up right behind the center is the quarterback. He handles the ball on almost every play, taking it from the center, then handing it to one of the other backs, throwing a pass or even keeping the ball and running with it.

Two other backs are positioned deeper and to the sides. They are called running backs.

The fourth back is stationed off to one side. His job is to receive passes. He is a second wide receiver.

Backs and pass receivers are smaller than linemen but they're also quicker and faster. Tony Dorsett of the Dallas Cowboys, one of the best running backs of the 1980s, was 5-foot-11 and weighed 185 pounds. That's not very big for pro football. But Dorsett was quick and very powerful, and able to explode through the smallest opening in the line.

In earlier days, the backfield was made up of a quarterback, two halfbacks, and a fullback. Football was much more of a running game in those days, and the backfield men either carried the ball or blocked. In college and high school play, the terms halfback and fullback are still used.

Teams use many variations of the offensive formation discussed here. A team may put two wide receivers on the same side of the line. The idea is to attack a weak spot in the defense.

A team may substitute a second tight end for one of the wide receivers. This makes for more blocking power in the line.

More and more, football is becoming a game in which there's a different formation for every situation. But the formation shown here is basic to every team's offense.

The Defensive Team

The defensive team has three layers. In front, right on the firing line, are the linemen. A few steps back are the linebackers.

The deepest defensive players are the cornerbacks and safeties. Together, these four players are known as the secondary.

The linemen have to be big and strong; in fact, they are usually the biggest and strongest men on the team. During the 1980s, the Dallas Cowboys pointed with pride to defensive end Ed (Too Tall) Jones. He stood 6-foot-9 and weighed 287 pounds.

Defensive linemen have to be quick, too. They have to be able to chase down the quarterback whenever he attempts a pass. The more time the passer has to scan the field and pick out a receiver, the greater the chance the pass is going to be completed.

The defensive linemen never stop trying to sack the quarterback. A sack is registered when a defensive player tackles the quarterback before he can get the ball away. Mark Gastineau, a defensive end for the New York Jets, was a master sacker. He once registered 22 sacks in a season, the all-time record.

The linebackers position themselves several yards behind the line. Linebackers have to combine power and speed. They need power to be able to dart forward and stop a runner dead in his tracks. They need speed to be able to drop back fast and defend against short passes.

Ed (Too Tall) Jones of the Dallas Cowboys towered over team's defensive coach, Ernie Stautner.

Defensive backs have to be quick and fast.

The cornerbacks are posted at the corners of the defensive formation. They're quick and fast. Their chief job is to defend against short passes, but they also must be able to rush forward and help bring down the ballcarrier.

The safeties are the deepest defensive backs, the last line of defense. They defend against long passes and also help out on running plays.

Defensive players generally line up in one of two different formations—the four-three formation or the three-four formation.

The four-three defense is made up of:

- Four linemen (two tackles, two ends)
- Three linebackers
- Two cornerbacks
- Two safeties

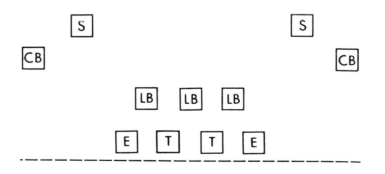

The four-three defense: two tackles (T), two ends (E), three linebackers (LB), two cornerbacks (CB), and two safeties (S)

The three-four defense consists of:

- Three linemen (two ends plus a nose tackle, also called a middle guard)
- Four linebackers
- Two cornerbacks
- Two safeties

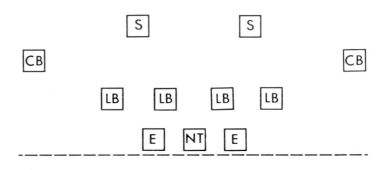

The three-four defense: two ends (E), a nose tackle (NT), four linebackers (LB), two cornerbacks (CB), and two safeties (S)

The linebackers and deep defensive backs use either zone coverage or man-to-man coverage in seeking to prevent passes from being completed. When using the zone system, each linebacker and defensive back is responsible for a certain area of the field. He covers any receiver who enters that area.

In man-to-man play, the defensive specialist covers a particular receiver. He stays with that man wherever he goes.

You also hear about double coverage. In this, two defensive players cover one receiver who is considered very dangerous.

The Lines of Scrimmage

The lines of scrimmage are two imaginary lines, each of which passes through a tip of the ball and runs parallel to the goal lines. The offensive and defensive teams face each other along these lines of scrimmage.

The area between the two scrimmage lines—which is the length of the ball—is called the neutral zone. No player other than the center is permitted to have any part of his body inside the neutral zone as the ball is being snapped.

The Kicking Game

Football involves two types of kicks and several different situations in which they are used. This stress on kicking is to be expected from a sport that has rugby and soccer in its background and *foot*ball for a name.

The two types of kicks are the punt and the place-kick. A punt is usually used on fourth down. The team in possession of the ball does not want to take

Wide receiver Phil McConkey (No. 80) of the Giants did double-duty as kick returner.

the risk of trying for a first down. The punter sends
the ball far downfield, hoping to back up the opposition against its own goal line.

A place-kick is used to put the ball in play at the
beginning of a half or after a touchdown or field goal,
or when attempting a field goal or a point after
touchdown.

When punting, the punter holds the ball in both
hands in front of his body, drops it and kicks it with
his instep before it hits the ground. A couple of fast
steps when executing the kick help to give height
and distance to the ball.

A skilled punter can kick the ball 60 or more yards.
But distance isn't the only factor to be considered in
judging a punt. The punter must also boot the ball
high. Coaches are concerned about "hang time"—
how long the ball remains in the air. The longer it's
up there, the better. The punting team wants as much
time as possible to gallop downfield to tackle the man
who catches the punt.

On a place-kick, the ball must be in contact with
the ground or supported by a tee when it is kicked.
If a tee is not used, a teammate of the kicker holds
the ball on end. Quarterbacks frequently serve as
ballholders.

There are two kinds of place-kickers. The most
numerous by far are soccer-style kickers. They ap-

Soccer-style place-kickers approach the ball diagonally, then plant nonkicking foot to one side of the ball.

proach the ball from an angle and boot it with one side of the instep.

The other method is to approach the ball head-on and kick it with the front end of the shoe.

The rules also permit a dropkick. In this, the kicker holds the ball end-down and lets it drop to the ground, kicking it just as it rebounds. No one dropkicks any more. In the days past, when the ball was rounded on the ends, the kicker was able to get a more reliable bounce than is possible with the pointy-ended ball in use today.

Special Teams

Besides offensive and defensive teams, there are also "special" teams. These are the teams that are on the field for punts, kickoffs, and field-goal and extra-point attempts. They are also called kicking teams.

Many players, however, refer to these teams as "suicide squads." That's because the injury rate is so high, six or seven times greater than on ordinary plays from scrimmage.

It's not hard to understand why special-team duty is so hazardous. Opposing special-team players often line up half-a-field apart. At the whistle, they rip toward each other at full throttle. Imagine two locomotives on the same track speeding toward each other. What happens if they meet? That gives you an idea of what special-team play is like.

It used to be that special teams were staffed only by rookies or soon-to-retire veterans. Not anymore. Even first-string players are given special-team duty nowadays. This is in addition, of course, to the regular role each man plays.

Players get assignments that match their skills. A speedster will be called upon to block the ball on punt or field-goal attempts. Good blockers are assigned to cut down opposition players on punt and kickoff returns.

Most special-team assignments require good speed and good size. And one other quality is a "must"— courage.

Plays and Strategy

The offensive team tries to gain yardage by means of plays. Each play is a carefully prepared action in which each player is given a specific set of duties to perform.

There are running plays and pass plays.

Some running plays seek to gain yardage by massing

physical power at the point of attack. For example, on a running play such as a sweep, both guards pull from their positions in the line and get out in front of the ballcarrier as he speeds to his left or right and then turns upfield.

With other plays, the offense tries to deceive the opposition. Take the draw play, for instance. The quarterback takes the snap and pedals back, his arm cocked as if he's going to pass. The defensive linemen rush in, intent on sacking him.

Suddenly the quarterback pulls the ball down and hands it to a running back. The back tucks the ball away and scurries right past the onrushing linemen.

This is called a draw play because the quarterback

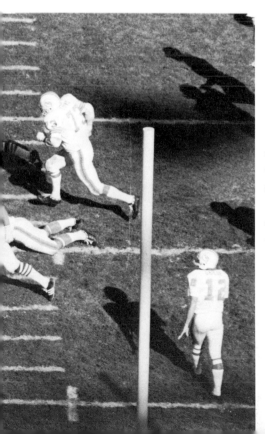

Miami Dolphins went undefeated in 1972, thanks to running plays like this sweep. Larry Csonka (39) carries the ball behind the blocking of running back Jim Kiick (21), tackle Doug Crusan (77), and guards Bob Kuechenberg (67) and Larry Little (66). Bob Griese (12) is the quarterback.

"draws" in opposing linemen before handing-off.

Most teams try to get their running game going first. Then, with the defense looking for a run, the quarterback starts throwing passes. If the defensive team has been caught off-guard, the aerial attack is almost certain to be successful.

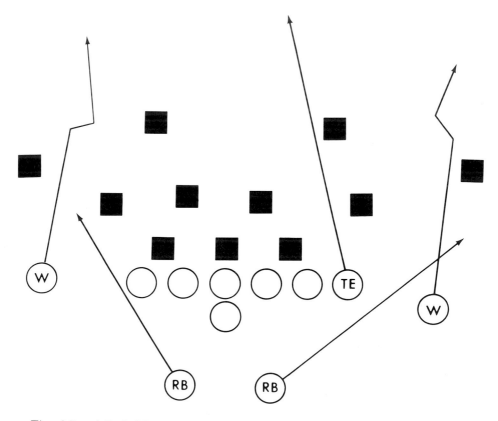

The Miami Dolphins sometimes used this all-purpose pass play. The wide receivers (W) and tight end (TE) are the primary receivers. If they're covered, the quarterback checks the running backs (RB); they're safety-valve receivers.

3

RULES TO REMEMBER

Football in the United States is played on many different levels. There is elementary school, high school, college, and professional football.

There are also independent football programs. One of the best known of these is the Pop Warner League for boys and girls, ages 7 to 16. Founded in Philadelphia in 1929, the Pop Warner football program became national in 1959.

Each level of football has its own rules.

Professional teams in the United States use the National Football League rulebook. In Canada, pro teams play by the rules of the Canadian Football League.

Most American college teams belong to either the National Collegiate Athletic Association or the National Association of Intercollegiate Athletics. The NCAA and NAIA set rules for their members.

Junior colleges and community colleges follow the

rules established by the National Junior College Athletic Association.

Most high schools play according to the rules of the National Federation of State High School Associations. The few high schools that haven't accepted the Association rulebook rely on the NCAA rules.

While the rules of play for each level are about the same, there are important differences. For example, a high school game lasts 48 minutes; professional and college games are 60 minutes in length.

The rules concerning timeouts are not all the same. In high school and college, four timeouts are permitted each half. In pro play, there can be only three timeouts each half. But the pro rules also permit several timeouts for television commercials.

Here's a rundown of football's most important rules.

Kicking Off

A kickoff starts each half of a football game. In pro football, the kickoff takes place from the kicking team's 35-yard line. In college and high school, the kickoff is made from the 40-yard line.

In pro ball, as well as in college and high school, once the ball travels 10 yards downfield, it is a free ball. Any player on any team may recover it.

A coin toss is used to decide which team will kick off. Team captains meet with the officials at the center

Kickoff coming up

Which team is to kick off? Coin toss decides.

of the field. The captain of the visiting team calls "heads" or "tails." The official tosses up the coin. The team that wins the toss has three choices:

1. Make the kickoff
2. Receive the kickoff
3. Choose the goal it wishes to defend

In almost every case, the team that wins the toss chooses to receive the kickoff, then tries to score. The other team gets to choose which goal it wishes to defend.

When the second half begins, the team that lost the coin toss before the game has the choice of kicking off, receiving, or defending either goal.

Once the ball has been placed on the kicking tee and is ready to be kicked, the kicker's teammates arrange themselves in a line across the field just behind the 35-yard line. (It's the 40-yard line in high school and college play.) They must remain behind the line until the ball is kicked.

Meanwhile, the receiving team places two fast and elusive runners near its goal line. The receiver who is nearest the ball will make the catch and run the ball back toward the other team's goal. His teammates will block for him.

The tension builds as the kickoff nears. With an upraised arm, the kicker signals that he's ready. The referee's whistle blasts. The game is underway. Every

On kickoff, Mark Collins of the Giants gathers in the ball and heads upfield as his blocking begins to form

pair of eyes is on the kicker as he approaches the ball, determined to drive it down field as far as he can.

Up into the air the ball arches. One of the receivers gathers it in. He starts upfield. He'll be happy if he can run the ball out to the 30-yard line. The kicking team wants to keep him inside the 25-yard line.

Bodies collide all over the field. You can hear the sharp *clack* of shell plastic hitting shell plastic. You hear loud grunts and groans.

The kick returner goes down, the victim of a lone tackler. An official takes the ball from the return man and places it at the point where the return ended.

The kickoff return team and the kickoff coverage team trickle toward the sidelines. Some of the players limp painfully. At the same time, the offensive and defensive teams swarm out onto the field.

If the kickoff soars beyond the end zone, or the receiver catches the ball in the end zone and makes no attempt to run it out of the end zone, he thereby "downs" the ball. This is a touchback. The receiving team then takes possession of the ball, first and 10 on its own 20-yard line.

If the kickoff goes out of bounds before it is touched and before it reaches the end zone, it must be kicked again. The kicking team is penalized five yards. When the ball is kicked again, it must be kicked from a point that is five yards closer to the kicking team's goal line.

In pro football, this means that the ball will be kicked from the 30-yard line instead of the 35-yard line.

Play of the Game

The offensive team has four plays, called downs, to move the ball at least 10 yards. When the offense gains 10 or more yards, it earns another first down. The team then gets four more downs to gain 10 more yards.

The ball is dead after every down, meaning it is temporarily out of play; it cannot be returned, kicked, or advanced. The clock may continue to run, however.

Before a play begins, the offensive team huddles. Usually only the quarterback speaks in the huddle. He announces the team's next play, the formation the team is to use and the signal on which the center is to snap the ball. The signal for the snap is usually a number or a color.

The defensive team may also huddle. In the defensive huddle, the captain of the defensive team announces the formation the team is to use.

The offensive team breaks from the huddle and lines up facing the defense. The quarterback bends over the center, calling the signals. When the ball snaps back from the center, the quarterback then hands the ball to a running back or pedals back several

Cardinal players hear the play from their quarterback.

steps and throws a pass. The quarterback can also keep the ball and run with it.

On a pass play, the quarterback retreats into what is called the pocket, a protective area formed by his tackles, guards, and the center. From within the pocket, the quarterback scans the area downfield, searching for an open receiver.

The passer must throw from behind the line of scrimmage. Only the ends and running backs are allowed to catch the pass.

The tackles, guards, and center must remain behind the line of scrimmage until the quarterback throws the ball. They then can race downfield and block for the receiver.

As the passer is getting set to throw, the defensive players start covering the receivers and backs. Once the ball is in the air, they seek to bat it down or, even better, catch it.

When a defensive player catches a pass, it is called an interception. The defensive player making the interception streaks for the opponent's goal line. Any player on the defensive team is eligible to intercept.

The defense can also gain possession of the ball by recovering a fumble. A fumble occurs when the ballcarrier drops the ball. But fumbles usually don't happen out of carelessness. Tacklers often try to strip the ball away, that is, tear it out of the ballcarrier's grasp.

In professional football, the defensive player recovering a fumble is permitted to run with it. But in college or high school, the defensive player can run with a fumble only if he catches it before it touches the ground. If he makes the recovery after the ball hits the ground, the team gets the ball at the spot where the recovery was made.

Substituting

Unlike baseball, which lives by pretty much the same rules year after year, football is a game that is constantly changing. One of the biggest changes has involved the right to substitute one player for another.

At one time, the rules limited the amount of substituting a coach could do. Almost everyone played on both offense and defense from the beginning of the game to the end.

Today, however, there is unlimited substitution. Suppose the Bears are playing the Cowboys. Whenever the Bears take over the ball, they send their 11-man offensive team into action. Dallas puts its defensive team on the field.

In addition, players with special talents are constantly going onto the field or coming off of it. A running back who has exceptional power may be put into the game when the team needs short yardage. A linebacker who is very fast will be used whenever the opposition is expected to pass.

As you can judge from all the players shuttling on and off the field, football is very much a game of specialists.

Punting

Again, suppose the Bears are playing the Cowboys. The game is scoreless. The Bears have tried three times to make a first down and have failed. They now have the ball on their own 28-yard line with 8 yards to go for a first down.

The Bears know that if they try for a first down a fourth time and fail, the Cowboys will take over the ball. That could hurt. The Dallas team will be very close to the Chicago end zone. A touchdown is a possibility. A field goal is almost a certainty.

Instead of taking the risk, the Bears punt. Their punter stands about 15 yards behind the line of scrimmage. This makes it difficult for the defensive players to block the kick.

Let's say he boots the ball 55 yards downfield. In other words, it comes down 40 yards from the line of scrimmage.

There a Dallas receiver raises one hand to signal a fair catch. He then makes the catch, ending the play. It is now the Cowboys' ball, first-and-10 on their own 32-yard line.

Punting is important. A team needs a good punter in order to be able to keep the opposition pinned down close to its own goal line.

A weak punt means trouble. It's almost like having a short pass intercepted.

These are the important punting rules:

The receiving team can catch the punt and run upfield with it. Or the receiving team can simply let the ball bounce and roll until it can bounce and roll no farther—it rolls "dead," in other words.

A third option the receiving team has is the fair catch. The receiver raises one hand, signaling a fair

A punt, kicked with the instep, demands a high-stepping kick like this one.

catch to the onrushing tackles, and then he catches the ball, which ends the play.

The idea of the fair catch is to give the receiving team the chance to save yardage by not letting the ball bounce or roll. The rules make it illegal for the defensive player to tackle or even touch the receiver making a fair catch. Since he is provided with this protection, the receiver has to give up the right to advance with the ball. The next play starts from the spot where the ball was caught.

A receiver attempting a fair catch has to be sure-handed. Should he fumble the catch, the ball can be recovered by the opposition.

The fair catch is used in situations where no advance seems possible. The tacklers have gotten downfield so quickly that they're practically breathing down the receiver's neck by the time the ball arrives.

If the punt goes out of bounds over a sideline, the ball is put in play on the yard line where it crossed the sideline.

If the receiver catches the ball in the end zone and makes no attempt to run it out, he thereby "downs" the ball. This is a touchback. The receiving team gets possession of the ball, first down on its own 20-yard line. A touchback also occurs when the ball goes beyond the end zone.

Of course, what the receiving team really hopes to do is run back the kick. A long runback wipes out the advantage the kicking team might have gained with a long punt. Occasionally you'll see a punt run back for a touchdown. It's one of football's most exciting plays.

About Time

Football, like basketball, hockey, or soccer, is a game that is played within a time limit. (Baseball, tennis, and golf do not have time limits.)

In college and professional football, a game lasts 60 minutes. The playing time of a high school game is 48 minutes.

The game is divided into halves. Each half is made up of two quarters, often called periods.

An intermission between halves, called half time, lasts fifteen minutes. There are also two-minute intermissions between the first two and last two quarters. Following each quarter, teams change goals.

In pro football, once the ball has been placed by the officials for the next play, the offensive team has 30 seconds to begin that play. It's 25 seconds in college and high school football. That's the amount of time the offensive team has to huddle, decide upon a play, call the play, line up at the line of scrimmage, call signals, and snap the ball.

Big 30-second clocks stand behind each end zone, where they can easily be seen by the quarterback as he hunches over the center and calls signals. Each clock reports the number of seconds remaining in digits that are several feet in height.

Stopping the Clock

While a pro or college game lasts 60 minutes, that means 60 minutes in which the ball is "in play." The official clock that registers those 60 minutes can be stopped for any of the following reasons:

- The ball carrier goes out of bounds
- A forward pass is incomplete
- A player is injured
- A score is made
- A penalty is called
- The officials need added time to get the ball "ready for play"
- A team calls a timeout.

There's another reason play can be stopped. In the case of games that are being televised, play is sometimes interrupted so the network can show a commercial.

In recent seasons, professional games being televised have included 25 commercial minutes. Many of the commercials are telecast during normal interruptions—when a timeout is called, after a touchdown or field goal, or when a penalty is called. But occasionally

---

PRO FOOTBALL'S LONGEST GAME

The longest pro football game ever played lasted 82 minutes, 40 seconds. A divisional playoff between the Kansas City Chiefs and the Miami Dolphins, the game was played at Municipal Stadium in Kansas City on Christmas Day, 1971.

At the end of four quarters, the game was tied, 24-24. Neither team managed to score in the fifth period.

Finally, after 7 minutes, 40 seconds of play in the sixth period, Miami's Garo Yepremian booted a 37-yard field goal, giving Miami a 27-24 victory.

---

play is halted by an official for the sole reason of allowing several commercials to be presented to the viewing audience.

Some people have objected to the interruptions for commercials. In fact, in a nationwide poll about football conducted by the *New York Times*/CBS not long ago, more people complained about commercials than anything else. Sixty percent said that they believed that "they [the networks] stop play too often just so they can show commercials."

Because official play is stopped so often, there is a big difference between actual playing time and elapsed time, the amount of time that actually passes during a game. The elapsed time of the 60-minute professional game is often more than three hours. A college game is closer to two-and-one-half hours.

4

ABOUT PENALTIES

The rules of football are very strict. Whenever a player breaks a rule—commits a foul, that is—his team must pay.

A foul is signaled by an official who throws a yellow cloth, or flag. The team that is guilty of committing the foul is penalized 5, 10, or 15 yards, depending on the kind of foul it is.

Fouls and Penalties

These are some of football's most common fouls, along with the penalty yards handed out for each:

Offside is called when an offensive or defensive player crosses the line of scrimmage before the ball is snapped. Penalty: 5 yards.

Holding is called when an offensive player uses his hands or arms to ward off a defensive player. Penalty: 10 yards.

A back judge (BJ), line judge (LJ), and field judge (FJ) take the field at Giants Stadium, East Rutherford, New Jersey.

There is also defensive holding, called when a defensive player holds or tackles anyone but the ballcarrier. Penalty: 5 yards. In professional football, defensive holding also means an automatic first down for the offense.

Clipping occurs when an offensive player blocks a defensive player from behind, especially by throwing his body across the back of the defensive player's legs. Penalty: 15 yards.

Roughing the passer is a foul committed by a defensive player who runs into or tackles the passer after the pass has been thrown. Penalty: 15 yards and an automatic first down.

Roughing the kicker is a foul committed by a defensive player who runs into or knocks down the kicker while he is punting or place-kicking. Penalty: 15 yards and an automatic first down.

Delay of game is the failure to put the ball in play within the time specified. In professional football the offensive team must put the ball in play within 30 seconds after the referee has signaled play to begin. In high school and college football, the interval is 25 seconds. Penalty: 5 yards.

Officials and Their Duties

It takes seven officials to supervise a pro football game and see to it that the rules are obeyed. These officials and their duties are as follows:

Referee—In charge of the game and has the final word on all rulings. When the ball is snapped, the referee stands behind the offensive backfield.

Umpire—Watches for rule violations at the line of

scrimmage. Positioned behind the defensive line. Also rules on players' equipment.

Head Linesman—Rules on offside and other violations before and as the ball is snapped. Stands at the end of the line of scrimmage. Also rules on sideline plays on his side of the field and supervises the sideline crew, the three men who keep track of the number of downs and the amount of yardage needed for a first down.

Line Judge—Positioned at the line of scrimmage on the side of the field opposite the head linesman.

"Second down" signals the head linesman.

Watches for offside and other violations before and as the ball is snapped. Serves as the official time-keeper, supervising the scoreboard clock.

Back Judge—Stationed behind the defensive secondary on the same side of the field as the line judge. Watches for violations involving pass receivers and defensive backs. Makes out-of-bounds rulings on his side of the field. With the field judge (see below), rules on whether field-goal and extra-point attempts are successful.

A field-goal attempt has gone wide is the official's signal here.

Line judge fires the pistol that ends each half.

Side Judge—Positioned opposite the back judge and on the same side of the field as the head linesman. Has the same responsibilities as the back judge.

Field Judge—Stands behind the defensive secondary at about the middle of the field. Watches the tight end and actions taken against him. Watches for violations on punt plays and deep passes. With the back judge, rules on whether field-goal and extra-point attempts are successful.

5

LOOKING BACK

In the beginning, football was a college game. Then high schools tried it. Colleges played football for more than half a century before the first professional league was formed.

Historians say that the first college football game was played on November 6, 1869. The scene was New Brunswick, New Jersey. Rutgers University faced the College of New Jersey (now Princeton University). Admission was free. About two hundred spectators showed up.

There were no uniforms. Despite a chilly wind, the twenty-five players on each side simply shed their coats, vests, and hats.

The game that was played that day closely resembled today's soccer. A round ball was used. Running with the ball or throwing it was not permitted. Holding and tripping were also forbidden.

But the game did have a few football-like qualities.

In earlier times, football was even more violent than it is today.

Players could catch the ball or bat it with their hands, unlike soccer. And running interference, that is, creating running room for the player with the ball at his feet, was permitted.

A goal, which had to be kicked, counted one point. Rutgers won the game by a score of 6 to 4.

Other Eastern schools took up the soccerlike game. One was Harvard. In 1874, Harvard, in Cambridge,

Massachusetts, played host to a Canadian team from McGill University in Montreal.

There was a debate over the rules that were to be used. Harvard wanted to play its soccerlike game. But McGill preferred to play the English game of rugby, which provided for catching and running with an egg-shaped ball.

The two teams worked out a settlement. They would play two games. In the first, they'd use Harvard's rules; in the second, McGill's.

The Harvard players liked McGill's rugby game so much that they embraced it as their own. Soon other Eastern colleges began playing rugby-style football, running and tackling instead of kicking. This was the start of football as we know it today.

Changing the Rules

In the years that followed, important changes were made in the rules of the game. Many of these changes were based upon the ideas of Walter Camp, who played football for Yale University from 1876 to 1882.

Camp pioneered the concept of having a quarterback handle the ball on every play. He was also responsible for introducing the system of downs. If a team couldn't gain a certain number of yards in a certain number of plays, it had to give up the ball to

COLLEGE FOOTBALL CONFERENCES

Most major colleges and universities compete within athletic associations called conferences. Each conference is usually made up of teams from the same geographic area. Teams within the same conference play each other during the season for the championship. The leading conferences include:

ATLANTIC COAST CONFERENCE

Clemson
Duke
Georgia Tech
Maryland
North Carolina
North Carolina State
Virginia
Wake Forest

IVY LEAGUE

Brown
Columbia
Cornell
Dartmouth
Harvard
Pennsylvania
Princeton
Yale

SOUTHEASTERN CONFERENCE

Alabama
Auburn
Florida
Georgia
Kentucky
Louisiana State
Mississippi
Mississippi State
Tennessee
Vanderbilt

BIG EIGHT CONFERENCE

Colorado
Iowa State
Kansas
Kansas State
Missouri
Nebraska
Oklahoma
Oklahoma State

the other team at the spot of the last "down." (A play was called a down because it ended where the ball-carrier was brought "down," that is, tackled.)

Despite the improvements, early football was a crude and violent sport. There were no penalties to

WESTERN ATHLETIC CONFERENCE

Air Force
Brigham Young
Colorado State
Hawaii
New Mexico
San Diego State
Texas (at El Paso)
Utah
Wyoming

PACIFIC TEN CONFERENCE

Arizona
Arizona State
California (at Berkeley)
Oregon
Oregon State
Stanford
UCLA (University of California
    at Los Angeles)
USC (University of Southern
    California)
Washington
Washington State

BIG TEN CONFERENCE

Illinois
Indiana
Iowa
Michigan
Michigan State
Minnesota
Northwestern
Ohio State
Purdue
Wisconsin

SOUTHWEST ATHLETIC CONFERENCE

Arkansas
Baylor
Houston
Rice
SMU (Southern Methodist
    University)
Texas
Texas A&M
Texas Christian
Texas Tech

Teams that do not belong to conferences are known as independent teams. Some of the leading independents are Army, Navy, Notre Dame, Penn State, and Pittsburgh.

curb roughness. So-called wedge plays were common. Blockers would align themselves in a V-formation, with the ballcarrier in the center of the V. When the ball was snapped, the point of the V would be "aimed" at a particular player or a hole in the line.

The brutality of wedge plays and the absence of penalties resulted in frequent injuries to players, even deaths. A crisis came in 1905, a year the football death toll reached eighteen.

President Theodore Roosevelt called college football leaders to the White House for a conference. "Clean up the game or abandon it," the president told them.

Out of the conference came new rules that made the game safer. One of these rules was based on an idea of John Heisman's. Heisman was a college player and later a noted coach. (The Heisman Memorial Trophy, awarded to the outstanding college football player each year, is named in honor of John Heisman.)

At the time, the football could be passed only across the field or backward (as in rugby). Heisman proposed passing the ball forward, too. Forward passing would help to make the game less violent, Heisman believed.

The rule-makers agreed. The forward pass was made legal in 1906.

Another rule adopted that year said that at least seven men had to be at the line of scrimmage when the center snapped the ball back. This rule helped to put an end to wedge formations.

Yale was the first major team to use the forward pass. In Yale's game against Harvard in 1906, neither team could score. Finally, Yale tried a pass—and it worked. Yale won, 6–0.

BIGGEST COLLEGE FOOTBALL STADIUMS

NAME, SCHOOL, LOCATION	SEATING CAPACITY
1. Michigan Stadium, University of Michigan, Ann Arbor	101,701
2. Neyland Stadium, University of Tennessee, Knoxville	91,246
3. Stanford Stadium, University of Stanford, Stanford, California	86,055
4. Ohio Stadium, Ohio State University, Columbus	85,290
5. Beaver Stadium, Penn State University, University Park	83,770
6. Sanford Stadium, University of Georgia, Athens	82,122
7. Memorial Stadium, University of Texas, Austin	80,000
8. Memorial Stadium, Clemson University, Clemson, South Carolina	79,725
9. Camp Randall, University of Wisconsin, Madison	77,280
10. Tiger Stadium, Louisiana State University, Baton Rouge	76,869

Passing helped to make football much more popular. Using the pass, a team of smaller, lighter players could compete at least on even terms with the heavier squad. Not only did the pass make football a more balanced game, it also made it more exciting. There were still plunges and pileups, of course, but they were far fewer in number.

Football continued to grow in popularity until World War I, which forced cutbacks in the sport. But in 1918, after the war, college football boomed in popularity once more.

Action in the Big Eight Conference, Nebraska vs. Kansas State

The enormous crowds that turned out for games enabled colleges to build huge stadiums. The income from football also allowed colleges to support many other sports—soccer, swimming, and track and field, for instance—which lacked spectator interest and thus were not able to pay for themselves.

MAJOR BOWL GAMES

At the end of the regular college football season, many college teams are invited to play in "bowl" games. The term comes from the fact that these games are often played in stadiums that are shaped like deep, rounded dishes—or "bowls." Bowl games are also played between teams of specially invited players.

Here is a list of the major bowl games (the dates indicate the year each game was first played).

Rose Bowl, Pasadena, California—1902
Orange Bowl, Miami—1935
Sugar Bowl, New Orleans—1935
Sun Bowl, El Paso, Texas—1936
Cotton Bowl, Dallas—1937
Gator Bowl, Jacksonville, Florida—1946
Florida Citrus Bowl, Orlando, Florida 1947
Bluebonnet Bowl, Houston—1959
Liberty Bowl, Memphis, Tennessee—1959
Peach Bowl, Atlanta—1968
Fiesta Bowl, Tempe, Arizona 1971
Independence Bowl, Shreveport, Louisiana—1976
All-American Bowl, Birmingham, Alabama—1977
Holiday Bowl, San Diego, California—1978
California Bowl, Fresno, California—1981
Aloha Bowl, Honolulu, Hawaii—1982
Freedom Bowl, Anaheim, California—1984

The Pro Game

Professional football, which today means the National Football League, grew out of the college game. The pros took the college rules and made them their own.

They took the college players and borrowed the college playing fields. They even took the college half-time show, the marching bands.

All of this began happening in the 1890s on the back lots of small towns in Pennsylvania and the Midwest.

The first teams were made up of college players who played for their schools on Saturday and as professionals on Sunday. A star player might earn as much as $100 for an afternoon of work.

Pro football was much different in those days. There was no time for practice. Plays and signals were put together in hurried meetings before the game. A uniform had to last an entire season.

There were no fancy stadiums. Fans would ring the playing field, standing two or three deep. Some spectators would watch from parked automobiles. A touchdown for the home team was often hailed by an explosion of sound from automobile horns.

Nobody ever boasted about being a pro player. It was a part-time job, something like working in a Burger King.

The game's only "name" player was Jim Thorpe, a hero of the 1912 Olympics, called by *The New York Times* the "athlete of the age." Thorpe signed in 1915 to play for the Canton Bulldogs. Thorpe was the game's biggest drawing card for years.

Jim Thorpe, pro football's first "name" player

Getting Organized

In the fall of 1920, the owners of eleven clubs met in Canton, Ohio, and formed the first league. It was called the American Professional Football Association. These were the teams:

Akron (Ohio) Pros
Canton (Ohio) Bulldogs
Cleveland (Ohio) Indians
Dayton (Ohio) Triangles
Decatur (Illinois) Staleys
Hammond (Indiana) Pros
Muncie (Indiana) Flyers
Racine Cardinals (from Chicago)
Rochester (New York) Jeffersons
Rock Island (Illinois) Independents

The membership fee, that is, the cost of a franchise, was $100. Today, of course, it costs tens of millions of dollars to buy a football franchise. The owners named Jim Thorpe to be the league's first president.

In 1922, the American Professional Football Association reorganized and changed its name to the National Football League. It expanded from eleven to eighteen teams. But they were still located mostly in small towns—in Rock Island, Illinois; Racine, Wisconsin; Evansville and Hammond, Indiana; and the like.

There were few glory days for the pro game during the 1930s. The country was gripped by the Great Depression. Employment was at a low ebb as economic activity shrank. Football franchises folded. In

1932, the NFL played with eight teams, the lowest number in history.

During the 1930s, pro football discovered the forward pass. Changes were made in the rules that made it easier for quarterbacks to throw passes. The changes opened the way for Sid Luckman of the Chicago Bears, Sammy Baugh of the Washington Redskins, and other great passers.

The Television Era

From the first days of football, the only way that a fan of a team could enjoy a game was by going to the stadium. There was no way to watch the team play when it traveled to a distant city for a game. You had to read the results in the newspaper the next day or listen to the game on the radio.

Radio broadcasts of football games are not very enjoyable. Radio is better for baseball. The pitcher throws, the batter swings, the fielder makes the play. Baseball unfolds like a story.

Not football. Football is masses of men all in action at once. It is impossible for the radio announcer to describe everything that happens.

Football is better suited for television. The first football game to be televised was played on Randall's Island in New York City on September 30, 1939, between Fordham University and Waynesburg (Penn-

BIGGEST FOOTBALL STADIUMS

NAME, LOCATION	SEATING CAPACITY
1. Rose Bowl, Pasadena, California	106,721
2. John F. Kennedy Stadium, Philadelphia, Pennsylvania	105,000
3. Los Angeles Memorial Coliseum	92,516
4. Pontiac Silverdome, Pontiac, Michigan	80,638
5. Rich Stadium, Buffalo, New York	80,290
6. Cleveland Municipal Stadium, Cleveland, Ohio	80,098
7. Arrowhead Stadium, Kansas City, Missouri	78,067
8. Giants Stadium, East Rutherford, New Jersey	76,891
9. Orange Bowl, Miami, Florida	75,500
10. Legion Field, Birmingham, Alabama	75,412

sylvania) College. The contest was televised by station WZXBS of New York. Fordham won, 34-7

Several weeks after the first college game was televised, TV discovered pro football. The first NFL game to be televised was played on October 22, 1939, at Ebbets Field in Brooklyn. The Brooklyn Dodgers, named for the Dodgers of baseball fame, defeated the Philadelphia Eagles, 23-14.

TV and pro football blossomed in the years after World War II. With its split-screen images, stop action, and instant replays, television helped viewers understand what was going on down on the field. Former football players and coaches explained plays and tactics.

Sammy Baugh, one of the pro game's first great passers

Television "discovered" football in the years following World War II, helping to broaden game's popularity.

Television triggered a period of tremendous growth for pro football. Even the tiniest towns came to have dedicated football fans. The fees paid by the television networks to the NFL brought prosperity to every team.

The popularity of pro football continued to grow, thanks to the American Football League, which began play in 1960. AFL teams played a wide-open brand of football, with daring passing. The AFL's New York

This bowl-shaped device, made of clear plastic and called a parabola, collects background sounds for TV audiences, adding to realism of telecasts.

American Football League operated for a ten-year period beginning in 1960.

Jets had Joe Namath, one of the most exciting players in pro football history.

The Super Bowl

The two leagues warred for years. In June, 1966, they agreed to become one. Out of the merger agreement, a championship game was scheduled. The first of these games was played on January 15, 1967, at the Los Angeles Coliseum. The NFL's Green Bay Packers defeated the AFL's Kansas City Chiefs, 35-10.

Little by little, people began referring to the championship game as the Super Bowl. The name caught on. The fifth Super Bowl, in 1971, was the first to be officially given a Roman numeral. Once Super Bowl V became a fact, Super Bowls I, II, III, and IV were created.

The Super Bowl and television go together like fries and a Coke. In fact, year in and year out, the Super Bowl ranks as one of the most-watched television programs in America, if not *the* most-watched.

Today, the NFL is made up of 28 teams. Each team represents a different city or region in the United States.

The teams are divided into the American Football Conference and National Football Conference. Within each conference, there are three divisions—Eastern, Central, and Western.

During the regular season, each team plays a schedule of sixteen games, most of them within its division but some outside of it. The team that wins the championship of its division, and the next two teams in each conference with the best won-lost records, advance to a series of playoff games.

The playoffs determine the conference champions.

NATIONAL FOOTBALL LEAGUE

AMERICAN FOOTBALL CONFERENCE

EASTERN DIVISION	CENTRAL DIVISION	WESTERN DIVISION
Buffalo Bills	Cincinnati Bengals	Denver Broncos
Indianapolis Colts	Cleveland Browns	Kansas City Chiefs
Miami Dolphins	Houston Oilers	Los Angeles Raiders
New England Patriots	Pittsburgh Steelers	San Diego Chargers
New York Jets		Seattle Seahawks

NATIONAL FOOTBALL CONFERENCE

EASTERN DIVISION	CENTRAL DIVISION	WESTERN DIVISION
Dallas Cowboys	Chicago Bears	Atlanta Falcons
New York Giants	Detroit Lions	Los Angeles Rams
Philadelphia Eagles	Green Bay Packers	New Orleans Saints
St. Louis Cardinals	Minnesota Vikings	San Francisco 49ers
Washington Redskins	Tampa Bay Buccaneers	

These two teams then meet in the Super Bowl. The winner reigns as the NFL champion.

Pro Football in Canada

The Canadian Football League, with nine teams competing in two divisions, traces its beginnings to the Interprovincial Rugby Football Union, which was organized and began play in 1907. Rugby football was first played in Canada as early as 1865.

The division champions play for the league title. The winner receives the Grey Cup, a silver trophy first awarded in 1909 for "the rugby-football championship of Canada." In the past, Canadian college teams also competed for the Grey Cup. But today it's symbolic of the pro championship only.

CANADIAN FOOTBALL LEAGUE

EASTERN DIVISION	WESTERN DIVISION
Hamilton Tiger Cats	British Columbia Lions
Montreal Concordes	Calgary Stampeders
Ottawa Rough Riders	Edmonton Eskimos
Toronto Argonauts	Saskatchewan Roughriders
	Winnipeg Blue Bombers

The NFL went through some troubled times during the 1980s. After the first two games in 1982, the NFL players went on strike, the first strike in NFL history.

Play resumed later in the season but the schedule had to be shortened because of the strike.

Also in 1982, a second pro league, the United States Football League, rose up to challenge the NFL. After a bitter struggle, the league folded in 1986.

During the 1980s, ratings for televised football games began to dip. People complained that games were too long and that there were too many penalties. Sometimes it seemed that the officials had too much control over what was happening on the field.

Despite the problems, people continued to watch pro football more than any other sport. It's a good bet that the sport will remain No. 1 in popularity for years to come.

Teams of the United States Football League are now history.

6

FAVORITE PLAYERS

Not long ago, *The New York Times* and CBS combined to conduct a nationwide poll of football fans to find out their likes and dislikes.

The Dallas Cowboys were picked by the fans as their favorite football team. Dan Marino, quarterback for the Miami Dolphins, was named the favorite player among active players.

Among all players, active as well as retired, Joe Namath, one-time quarterback for the New York Jets, led the list. O. J. Simpson, the fast and elusive running back for the Buffalo Bills, and Roger Staubach, who quarterbacked the Dallas Cowboys during their years of glory, were tied for second place in the poll.

The pages that follow profile Namath, Simpson, and Staubach, as well as the other eight players the fans selected as their heroes.

As running back, Jim Brown rewrote the NFL record book.

Jim Brown

For the nine years he played for the Cleveland Browns of the National Football League, from 1957–1965, Jim Brown was the best running back in the game. He is often called the best running back in pro football history.

Brown, at 6-foot-2, 230 pounds, was a punishing runner who had unusual quickness to go with his tremendous power. Willie Davis, an All-Pro defensive end with the Green Bay Packers, once described what it was like to tackle Brown: "It was just me and him, one on one. Well, I hit him, hit him good, and we both went down. And it was one of the few times in my life when my whole body was aching. Only my pride made me get up."

Brown seldom showed any emotion during a game. Never complain; never explain. That was his style. Whether one man tackled him or a whole army, he would get up slowly to conserve his strength. He could be in agonizing pain but you could never tell it from his face. He never missed a game.

Born in Georgia, Brown grew up on Long Island, New York. He graduated from Manhasset High School in 1953 after winning 13 letters in five sports. At Syracuse University, he won All-America honors as a running back in football and as a midfielder in lacrosse.

Brown was the NFL's Rookie of the Year in 1957 and a Pro Bowl selection every year he played. He was the league's Most Valuable Player in 1957 and again in 1965.

Brown practically rewrote the NFL record manual. At the time he retired, he had gained a record 12,312 yards. The No. 2 man on the all-time rushing-yardage list was more than a mile behind him.

In the decades following his retirement, many of Brown's records were surpassed. (Walter Payton now holds the all-time rushing record.) Brown didn't like seeing his records wiped out. He felt that running backs of the 1970s and 1980s had it much easier than he did. Standards were different. When Brown played, the season was 12 games and later 14 games in length. The NFL started playing 16 games a season in 1978. The added games gave running backs many more opportunities to carry the ball.

In Brown's time, to gain 1,000 yards in a season was considered a notable feat. "Gaining 1,000 yards in a 16-game season," Brown once noted, "isn't even worth talking about."

Brown retired abruptly in 1965 to pursue a career in movies and television. The move surprised many people, who felt he had several good seasons left. "It was the right time to retire," he once said. "You have to go out on top."

Gale Sayers

Gale Sayers, who played for the Chicago Bears from 1965 through 1971, was one of the most remarkable open-field runners pro football has ever known. Fast

and powerful, he could stop and start, whirl and spin, and never lose his balance. He had tricky head, shoulder, hip, and leg fakes.

Sayers created a sensation during his rookie season, staging one spectacular performance after another. In a late-season game against the San Francisco 49ers, Sayers tied the all-time record by scoring six touchdowns. He might have scored a seventh if his coach had not rested him in the game's final minutes. Three of Sayers's scoring runs measured 50, 80, and 85 yards.

In all of pro football history, only two other men have scored six touchdowns in one game—Dub Jones of the Cleveland Browns in 1951, and Ernie Nevers of the Chicago Cardinals in 1929.

Nevers watched Sayers's six-touchdown game on television. Nevers was sixty-six years old at the time. "I've seen a lot of football," said Nevers. "I've seen a lot of players, but this was the best performance I've ever seen."

Sayers set another record during his rookie season by scoring 22 touchdowns. (That record was later topped by O. J. Simpson of the Buffalo Bills and John Riggins of the Washington Redskins.)

Sayers summed up his success in simple terms. "I

Sayers electrified fans during brief career.

just look for the hole," he said, "and let instinct get me loose."

Gale Sayers was born in Wichita, Kansas, on May 30, 1943. For a time, he lived on a farm near the town of Speed, Kansas. He grew up in Omaha, Nebraska, and attended high school there.

After he graduated, Sayers enrolled at the University of Kansas. His speed as a runner and his pass-catching ability earned him All-America honors.

At the time Sayers graduated, his coach said of him: "He was just great. Nobody in pro ball is going to catch him."

As a pro player, Sayers not only toiled as a running back and pass receiver, he also returned punts and kickoffs. During his career, he returned kickoffs for touchdowns six times, an NFL record.

Injuries ruined Sayers's career. He missed several games in 1968 after seriously damaging his right knee. The following year he led the NFL in rushing, with 1,032 yards gained.

But in 1970, he was cut down again. This time it was the "other" knee, the left knee, that was injured. He quit pro football early in 1972. Sayers was elected to Pro Football's Hall of Fame five years later.

Gale Sayers's career lasted only 68 games. He held some 20 Chicago Bears records at the time he retired. Were it not for those injuries, there's no telling what he might have accomplished.

George Blanda

Gray-haired, crinkly-faced George Blanda was a rarity in football. He was both a place-kicker and a quarterback. There's no one in the game today who plays both of those roles.

Blanda was also unusual because his career lasted such a long time. Blanda, in fact, played 26 years in the NFL, a record.

Blanda was born in Youngwood, Pennsylvania, on September 17, 1927. He graduated from the University of Kentucky in 1949, the same year he joined the Chicago Bears.

Blanda's pro career ended after the 1975 season, when he was forty-eight. (Blanda did not play in 1959.) He played for the Chicago Bears, Baltimore Colts, Houston Oilers, and Oakland Raiders.

Since Blanda was a place-kicker and quarterback, and played for more than 20 years, he had an opportunity to score a tremendous number of points—and he did. With 2,002 points, Blanda ranks as the No. 1 scorer in pro football history.

This is the way Blanda scored all those points:

Field goals, 335	1,005 points
Points after touchdown, 943	943 points
Touchdowns, 9	54 points

Blanda's career seemed at an end in 1958. The

Chicago Bears, the team he was playing for at the time, did not offer him a contract for the 1959 season.

But that was the year the American Football League began setting up shop. AFL teams needed experienced players. Blanda, a ten-year veteran, signed with the AFL's Houston franchise.

In 1961, Blanda was named the AFL's Most Valuable Player. It was the climax of one of the most successful comebacks in pro football history. Blanda became a member of the Pro Football Hall of Fame in 1981.

Bart Starr

During the decade of the 1960s, when professional football was becoming the nation's No. 1 sport, Bart Starr of the Green Bay Packers ranked as the game's No. 1 quarterback.

As a passer, Starr was very close to perfect. During the seasons of 1964 and 1965 he threw 294 consecutive passes without an interception. That's a record that still stands.

Starr was always quiet and determined. He quarterbacked the Packers to NFL championships in 1961, 1962, 1965, 1966, and 1967. He guided the team to victories in Super Bowl I and Super Bowl II. Although

Blanda starred as both a place-kicker and quarterback.

he was named the Most Valuable Player in both Super Bowls, the headlines usually went to Starr's more colorful teammates.

Whenever Starr completed an important pass, he gave credit to the receiver. In the NFL title game in 1967, Starr scored the winning touchdown on a bold, last-second decision to keep the ball and smash his way into the end zone. But afterward, the guard who blocked for him—Jerry Kramer—got most of the praise.

Bart Starr was born on January 9, 1934, in Montgomery, Alabama. After high school in Montgomery, Starr went to the University of Alabama. He joined the Packers in 1956. But he didn't become the team's starting quarterback until after Vince Lombardi took over as coach in 1959.

Lombardi was strict; he demanded much. Starr liked this. He praised Lombardi in glowing terms. "He is the man who taught me everything about football, about leadership, about life," Starr once said. "Everything I am as a man and as a football player, I owe to him."

Starr began having problems with his throwing arm in 1967. He retired as a player in 1971. Six years later, he was elected to the Pro Football Hall of Fame.

In 1974, Starr joined the Packers as the team's coach, a post he held until 1983. Unfortunately, his

Starr ranks as one of the most accurate passers of all time.

record as a coach never came close to equaling all
that he had achieved as a player.

Johnny Unitas

It is often called the "greatest football game ever played." It was the game to decide the 1958 championship of the National Football League, the Baltimore Colts vs. the New York Giants.

With two minutes to play, the Giants led, 17-14. It was Baltimore's ball on their own 14-yard line. In the huddle, Johnny Unitas, the Colts stony-faced quarterback, told his teammates: "This is where we find out what we're made of."

Unitas calmly tossed four passes that brought the Colts to the Giants 20-yard line. From there, the Colts kicked a field goal to tie the score.

In pro football's first sudden-death overtime, Unitas called short passes and smashes up the middle, quickly marching the Colts to the New York one-yard line. Fullback Alan Ameche then scored the winning touchdown.

Afterward, a reporter asked Unitas if his last pass hadn't been risky. "A pass," said Unitas, "is never risky when you know what you're doing."

In victory or defeat, Johnny Unitas was always cool and poised. "He's got ice water in his veins," a teammate once said of him.

Unitas was the Colts quarterback from 1956 through 1972. During that time, Baltimore won the NFL championship three times. They beat Dallas, 16-13,

Unitas awaits the call to action in Super Bowl III.

in Super Bowl V. Unitas was the league's Most Valuable Player twice, in 1964 and 1967.

A native of Pittsburgh, where he was born on May 7, 1933, Unitas played his college football at the

University of Louisville. After he failed a tryout with the Pittsburgh Steelers, he played a year of semi-pro football. He was paid $6 a game.

The Colts decided to take a chance on Unitas in 1956. Two years later, he led the team to the NFL title.

After his retirement, Unitas was a sportscaster for several years. He lived in Baltimore and did promotion work for a number of companies. He also operated a restaurant. It was aptly named. It was called The Golden Arm.

Dick Butkus

A big man at 245 pounds, and usually grim-faced, Dick Butkus, middle linebacker for the Chicago Bears, is said by many to be the best ever to play that very demanding position.

There is plenty of evidence to support that claim. Toward the end of Butkus's career, *Sport* magazine took a poll of NFL quarterbacks to find out which linebacker they "feared" the most. Getting the quarterbacks to say that they "feared" anyone was difficult. The most they would say is that they *respected* certain linebackers. And Dick Butkus was the linebacker they respected more than anyone else. Ten quarterbacks voted Butkus as being the best. Ten others said that he was one of the best. "The clear evidence," said

Butkus was a decisive factor in almost every game he played.

Sport, "is that Dick Butkus remains king of the hill."

It's no wonder that quarterbacks thought so highly of Butkus. He played every game at a fever pitch, combining a super sense of what was going on with the willingness to hurl his body at the point of attack. Butkus, in fact, thrived on body contact; he loved to hit.

With Butkus on the field, a quarterback had to think twice before sending a running play up the middle or pass into the zone that Butkus was covering. He made the offense adjust simply by being there. "The best way to play Dick Butkus," one quarterback said, "is to avoid him."

Butkus, one of eight children, was born in Chicago on December 9, 1942, and grew up there. He began playing football in eighth grade. When it came to pick a high school, Butkus chose Chicago Vocational. The reason: Because the school had a good football coach.

Later, at the University of Illinois, Butkus was an All-America performer and Lineman of the Year in 1964. After college, he signed a contract with the Chicago Bears worth $200,000. At the time, it was the most money ever paid to a defensive player.

At the end of his first year, Butkus won All-NFL honors as middle linebacker, an amazing achievement for a rookie. It usually takes at least two or three years to play the position well.

"There's only one thing I ever wanted to do," Butkus once said. "Play pro football. Everyone seems to be made for something. I've always felt that playing pro football was the thing I was supposed to do."

Someone once asked Butkus whether he was ever scared on a football field.

"Scared?" Butkus asked, his brow wrinkling. "Scared of what?"

Then he thought for a while. "Injuries," he said. "Just injuries. That's the only thing to be afraid of."

Injuries were what finally brought Butkus down. He required knee surgery in January, 1971, again in March of that year and many times thereafter. His battered knees became so misshapen that each looked like a bag of walnuts.

Butkus's bad knees eventually forced him out of the game. The season of 1973 was his last. After he retired, Butkus enjoyed a very successful career as a sportscaster and television actor.

Joe Namath

Author and *Sport* magazine editor John Devaney sat next to quarterback Joe Namath one spring afternoon in 1965 on a commercial jet plane bound for Birmingham, Alabama, from Chicago. They discussed how Namath, who had recently graduated from the University of Alabama and signed a $400,000 contract with the New York Jets, was going to perform as a pro player.

"Just write this down," said Namath, jabbing one of his long fingers at Devaney's notebook. "Take everything into account," said Namath, "my injury, all the publicity, all the pressure and just throw them away, because I'm going to make it."

Namath, who was born in Beaver Falls, Pennsyl-

Namath was always colorful even in choice of headgear.

vania, on May 31, 1943, the son of a steel-mill worker, did much more than "make it." Thanks to his strong and accurate right arm, and the quick way in which he released the ball, Namath is hailed as one of the best passers in pro football history. Cool and confident under pressure, he was also often described as being the game's No. 1 quarterback in terms of his ability to move a team.

Namath had some exceptional days as a pro. Twice during the season of 1972, Namath passed for 400 or more yards in a game. One of those games was against the Oakland Raiders. "He was like a magician out there," said an Oakland player afterward. "He was unreal."

Namath steered the Jets to the championship of the old American Football League in 1968. That earned the Jets the right to meet the Baltimore Colts for the pro football championship. (Later, the game would be named Super Bowl III.) No AFL team had ever defeated an NFL team in championship play. That didn't bother Namath. "We're going to beat the Colts on Sunday," he announced the week before the game. "I *guarantee* it!"

Namath was close to perfect that day, mixing running plays with pinpoint passes. The Jets won, 16-7, in what is often termed the biggest upset in Super Bowl history.

That game was the high-water mark for Namath.

He had bad knees and wasn't able to duck onrushing defensive players. He was injured several times as a result. He missed many games during the seasons of 1970, 1971, and 1973.

During the eight seasons that followed the New York team's Super Bowl victory, the Jets had only one winning season. Namath's overall record was 60 wins, 63 losses, and 4 ties.

But few people remember that Namath had a losing record as a pro player. And those who do remember don't care. Namath predicted a victory for the Jets in the Super Bowl, and then he went out and made that prediction come true. That will never be forgotten.

In 1977, the Jets traded Namath to the Los Angeles Rams. He played little. At the end of the season he announced his retirement. He appeared in a handful of movies and on the Broadway stage and also worked as a television sportscaster. Namath was elected to the Pro Football Hall of Fame in 1985.

Roger Staubach

During most of the 1960s, the Dallas Cowboys were often called "next year's champions." They were always the team that was supposed to win the National Football League championship—but they were never able to.

Then along came Roger Staubach. In 1971, his first year as the starting quarterback for the Cowboys, Staubach guided the team to the division title and into the Super Bowl, where they turned back the Miami Dolphins, 24-3.

Staubach completed 12 of 19 passes that day, two of which resulted in touchdowns. He was named the game's Most Valuable Player.

So began an era of championship seasons for the Dallas Cowboys. Throughout the rest of Staubach's career, which ended in 1981, the Dallas team failed to make the play-offs only once.

Staubach made three more Super Bowl appearances with the Cowboys. He led the team to a victory over the Denver Broncos in Super Bowl XII. In the other two Super Bowls, the Cowboys were edged out by Terry Bradshaw and the Pittsburgh Steelers. After Roger retired, the Cowboys again found success difficult to achieve.

Staubach wasn't a bad passer and he liked to run with the ball when pressured by the defense. But he won the most praise for his leadership skills—his maturity, his confidence.

His ability as a leader was developed during the four years Staubach attended the U.S. Naval Academy at Annapolis. As the quarterback for the Academy team, Staubach won the Heisman Trophy in 1963.

Staubach targets on a favorite receiver.

After graduation, Roger fulfilled a four-year commitment as a naval officer. He was twenty-seven years old when he joined the Cowboys in 1969.

Staubach was born in Cincinnati (on February 5, 1942) and brought up there. After he retired from pro football, he lived in Dallas, where he was active in the real estate business.

Staubach was elected to the Pro Football Hall of Fame in 1985. He and O. J. Simpson are the only Heisman Trophy winners to have been named to the Canton, Ohio, shrine.

O. J. Simpson

Noted for his speed and the twisting, darting way he ran, O. J. Simpson ranks as one of the best runners in football history. The "O. J." stands for Orenthal James, but everyone called him The Juice.

Simpson was born in San Francisco on July 9, 1947. His family lived in a public housing project in the Portrero Hill section of the city.

Simpson was an outstanding high school athlete but his grades weren't good enough to enable him to go to a major college. O. J. went to a junior college instead, where he became a football star. He later attended the University of Southern California. In 1968, Simpson won the Heisman Trophy as the nation's best college player.

Simpson takes time out for a water break.

O. J. was drafted by the Buffalo Bills, one of the worst teams in pro football at the time. The Bills managed to win only eight games in O. J.'s first three years with the team. They were often unhappy years for O. J.

Not until 1972 did O. J. begin to shine. That year he gained 1,251 yards to lead the league.

In 1973, O. J. was even better. He ended the season with 2,003 yards, the all-time season's record. (The record was broken by Eric Dickerson of the Los Angeles Rams in 1984.) O. J. was named the NFL's

Player of the Year that year, 1973, and again in 1975.

Simpson's name was in the headlines again in 1976. He gained a record 273 yards in a game against the Detroit Lions. (Walter Payton of the Chicago Bears broke that record in 1977.)

"I don't feel I have to challenge tacklers," O. J. once said. "I ran a lot by instinct and how much I can see when I'm through the hole."

Simpson retired after the season of 1979 and became a television sports commentator. He lived in Beverly Hills, California. In 1985, he was named to the Pro Football Hall of Fame.

Terry Bradshaw

Terry Bradshaw of the Pittsburgh Steelers is ranked with football's greatest quarterbacks. Like Joe Namath, Bradshaw was a strong-armed and accurate passer. Like Bart Starr, he was a cool play-caller. The powerful Bradshaw was also good at running with the ball.

No other quarterback can match Bradshaw's record of having been the winning quarterback on four Super Bowl teams. For his performance in Super Bowl XIII in 1979 and Super Bowl XIV in 1980, Bradshaw was named the game's Most Valuable Player.

Terry Bradshaw was born in Shreveport, Louisiana, on September 2, 1948. Because the weather is warm there most of the time, Terry played sports the year 'round—baseball in the spring and summer, football in the fall and winter.

Terry's favorite football player was Johnny Unitas, the star quarterback of the Baltimore Colts. Terry watched Unitas on television. Unitas was Terry's idol because he not only passed the ball, he ran with it. Terry wanted to be an all-around player.

In high school, Terry was the team's strong-armed quarterback. His coach praised his long passes. "They go like they're shot from a cannon," he said.

In college, at Louisiana Tech, Terry's bullet passes paced the team to the conference championship.

Terry was drafted by the Pittsburgh Steelers in 1969. The team had won only one game that season. Never had the Steelers won a championship.

Terry predicted he would have the Steelers playing in the Super Bowl right away. It was a foolish prediction. The Steelers had losing records in 1970 and 1971.

But all the while, Bradshaw was improving. He learned to "read" pro defenses. He became a better play-caller.

In 1973 and 1974, the Steelers qualified for the play-offs. In 1975, Bradshaw led the team into the Super Bowl for the first time. They beat the Minnesota Vikings, 16-6. Afterward a teammate hugged Terry

Terry Bradshaw, the winning quarterback on four Super Bowl teams.

and said, "You said five years ago we'd do it—and we did!"

One successful year followed another. Bradshaw steered the Steelers into four Super Bowls—in 1975,

1976, 1979, and 1980. The Steelers won every one. No other team has captured four Super Bowls.

Bradshaw set Super Bowl records that still stand. In Super Bowl XIV in 1979, in which the Steelers defeated the Los Angeles Rams, 31-19, Terry threw a record four touchdown passes.

He also holds these Super Bowl records:

- Most Yards Gained Lifetime, 932
- Most Touchdown Passes, Lifetime, 9

Bradshaw was interested in country-and-western music. He once made a record that was titled "I Get So Lonesome I Could Cry." He planned to get serious about a career in music after he retired. Instead, he became a television sports commentator. He was often seen on national football telecasts.

Walter Payton

On the morning of November 20, 1977, running back Walter Payton of the Chicago Bears awoke feeling weak and wobbly from the flu. He wasn't very cheerful about the game with the Minnesota Vikings scheduled that afternoon.

In the game's first half, Payton showed no effects of the flu. He spearheaded the Chicago attack. The Bears took a 10-0 lead.

Payton rushed for 144 yards in that first half. Some

people thought he might threaten the NFL's record of 273 yards in a game. The record was held by O. J. Simpson.

But the Vikings held Payton in check for most of the second half. He gained only 66 yards. That gave Payton 210 yards for the day. Simpson's record seemed safe.

Suddenly, with only minutes left to play, Payton broke loose, galloping for a 58-yard gain. Now he needed only six more yards to break the record. He gained seven yards on his final two carries. The record was his.

Payton's statistics for the game included 40 carries, 275 yards, and a 6.9 rushing average. Not bad for a flu victim. The Bears won the game, 10-7.

Walter Payton, a star running back at Jackson (Mississippi) State University before he joined the Chicago Bears in 1975, made a habit of setting records. Strong and durable, he became the leading rusher in NFL history in 1984. He did so by breaking Jim Brown's career rushing record of 12,312 yards. By the end of the 1986 season, Payton's career rushing total had reached 16,193 yards.

Walter Payton was born in Columbia, Mississippi, in 1954. His father, a factory worker, always told him to "be the best." That idea would stay with Walter throughout his life.

Walter developed his never-say-die running style

during his high school years. Sometimes he gallops into would-be tacklers. Other times he tries to leap over them. He is also a fearsome blocker and sure-handed receiver.

In 1977, thanks mostly to Payton's remarkable running and pass receiving, the Bears posted their first winning season in ten years. In 1985, the team finished with a 15-1 record.

They then smothered the New England Patriots in Super Bowl XX, 46-10. Payton carried the ball 22 times for 61 yards.

Payton was one of the highest paid players in pro football. In 1983, he signed a contract with the Bears that guaranteed him $240,000 *for life*.

Nobody ever said that Payton was paid too much. An opposition player once remarked that tackling Payton was like "trying to rope a calf."

"Amazing" is the word a teammate once used in describing him. "He has the ability to come up with the big play each week," the teammate said. "He does things nobody else can do."

Quick and powerful, Chicago's Walter Payton holds NFL's all-time rushing record

FOOTBALL WORDS AND TERMS

Blitz—An all-out rush by one or more linebackers and defensive backs. They charge through the offensive line and try to sack the quarterback before he can pass or hand off the ball.

Completion—A pass that is legally caught.

Down—An offensive play which begins with a center snap and ends when the ball becomes dead.

Extra Points—One point can be earned by a team for a successful place-kick after the team has scored a touchdown. In high school and college football, two points are awarded for running or passing the ball across the goal line following a touchdown.

Fair Catch—A catch of a punted ball in which the receiver signals (by means of an upraised hand) that he will not advance the ball after the catch. A receiver making a fair catch cannot be interfered with or tackled.

Field Goal—Three points, earned when a place-kick goes over the opposition crossbar and between the uprights of the opposition goalposts.

Field Position—The location of the ball on the field. When the offense has the ball near the opposition's goal line, it is said to have "good" field position.

Formation—The way in which the offensive or defensive team lines up at the beginning of each play.

Forward Pass—A ball thrown toward the opposition goal line.

Fumble—A ball in play that is dropped or otherwise becomes loose.

Incomplete—A forward pass that is not caught or intercepted.

Interception—A forward pass caught by the defense (which then becomes the offense).

Lateral—A pass thrown in any direction except toward the opposition's goal line.

Line of Scrimmage—One of two imaginary lines, each of which passes through a tip of the ball and runs parallel to the goal lines. Opposing teams line up on these lines.

Pass Rush—The attempt by the defensive team to tackle the quarterback before he can throw the ball.

Penalty—The punishment for breaking a rule. Usually the penalized team is set back 5 to 15 yards, but a penalty can also involve the loss of a down or possession of the ball.

Place-kick—A kick made while the ball is in contact with the ground, that is, held on end by a teammate of the kicker, or placed on a kicking tee.

Punt—A kick from scrimmage in which the ball is dropped from the hands and kicked before it hits the ground.

Recover—To gain possession of a fumbled ball.

Rush—To run with the ball on a play from scrimmage.

Sack—To tackle the quarterback before he can throw a pass.

Safety—The two points that are awarded a team that forces the opposition to down the ball behind its goal line.

Snap—The action of the center in which he hands or passes the ball back between his legs to the quarterback, ballholder, or punter to begin a play.

Touchback—For a team to gain possession of the ball in the end zone it is defending on a play in which the opposition team caused the ball to cross the goal line (as when the ball is punted). The team gaining possession of the ball begins the next play from its 20-yard line.

Touchdown—Six points, earned by carrying the ball into or catching a forward pass in the opposition's end zone.

ALL-TIME RECORDS

Scoring Records

Most Points, Career—2,002, George Blanda, Chicago Bears, Baltimore Colts, Houston Oilers, Oakland Raiders, 1949–1975

Most Points, Season—176, Paul Hornung, Green Bay Packers, 1960

Most Points, Game—40, Ernie Nevers, Chicago Cardinals vs. Chicago Bears, Nov. 28, 1929

Most Touchdowns, Career—126, Jim Brown, Cleveland Browns, 1957–1965

Most Touchdowns, Season—24, John Riggins, Washington Redskins, 1983

Most Touchdowns, Game—6, Ernie Nevers, Chicago Cardinals vs. Chicago Bears, Nov. 28, 1929; Dub Jones, Cleveland Browns vs. Chicago Bears, Nov. 25, 1951; Gale Sayers, Chicago Bears vs. San Francisco 49ers, Dec. 12, 1965

Rushing Records

Most Yards Gained, Career—16,193, Walter Payton, Chicago Bears, 1975–1986

Most Yards Gained, Season—2,105, Eric Dickerson, Los Angeles Rams, 1984

Most Yards Gained, Game—275, Walter Payton, Chicago Bears vs. Minnesota Vikings, Nov. 20, 1977

Most Touchdowns, Rushing, Career—106, Jim Brown, Cleveland Browns, 1957–1965

Most Touchdowns, Rushing, Season—24, John Riggins, Washington Redskins, 1983

Most Touchdowns, Rushing, Game—6, Ernie Nevers, Chicago Cardinals vs. Chicago Bears, Nov. 28, 1929

Longest Run from Scrimmage—99 yards, Tony Dorsett, Dallas Cowboys vs. Minnesota Vikings, Jan. 3, 1983

Passing Records

Most Yards Gained, Career—47,003, Fran Tarkenton, Minnesota Vikings, New York Giants, 1961–1978

Most Yards Gained, Season—5,084, Dan Marino, Miami Dolphins, 1984

Most Yards Gained, Game—554, Norm Van Brocklin, Los Angeles Rams vs. New York Yankees, Sept. 28, 1951

Most Touchdown Passes, Career—342, Fran Tarkenton, Minnesota Vikings, New York Giants, 1961–1978

Most Touchdown Passes, Season—48, Dan Marino, Miami Dolphins, 1984

Most Touchdown Passes, Game—7, Sid Luckman, Chicago Bears vs. New York Giants, Nov. 14, 1943; Adrian Burk, Philadelphia Eagles vs. Washington Redskins, Oct. 17, 1954; George Blanda, Houston Oilers vs. New York Titans, Nov. 19, 1961; Y. A. Tittle, New York Giants vs. Washington Redskins, Oct. 28, 1962; Joe Kapp, Minnesota Vikings vs. Baltimore Colts, Sept. 28, 1969

Most Consecutive Passes Completed—20, Ken Anderson, Cincinnati Bengals vs. Houston Oilers, Jan. 2, 1983

Pass Receiving Records

Most Pass Receptions, Career—716, Charlie Joiner, Houston Oilers, Cincinnati Bengals, San Diego Chargers, 1969–1985

Most Pass Receptions, Season—106, Art Monk, Washington Redskins, 1984

Most Pass Receptions, Game 18, Tom Fears, Los Angeles Rams vs. Green Bay Packers, Dec. 3, 1950

Most Consecutive Games, Pass Receptions—127, Harold Carmichael, Philadelphia Eagles, 1972–1980

Pass Interception Records

Most Pass Interceptions, Career—81, Paul Krause, Washington Redskins, Minnesota Vikings, 1964–1979

Most Pass Interceptions, Season—14, Dick Lane, Los Angeles Rams, 1952

Most Pass Interceptions, Game—4, (16 players)

Punting Records

Highest Punting Average, Season—51.40 yards, Sammy Baugh, Washington Redskins, 1940

Longest Punt—98 yards, Steve O'Neal, New York Jets vs. Denver Broncos, Sept. 21, 1969

Punt Return Records

Most Yardage Returning Punts, Career—3,036, Billy Johnson,

Houston Oilers, Atlanta Falcons, 1974–1985

Most Yardage Returning Punts, Season—692, Fulton Walker, Miami Dolphins, Los Angeles Raiders, 1985

Most Yardage Returning Punts, Game—207, LeRoy Irvin, Los Angeles Rams vs. Atlanta Falcons, Oct. 11, 1981

Longest Punt Return—98 yards, Gil LeFebvre, Cincinnati Reds vs. Brooklyn Dodgers, Dec. 3, 1933; Charles West, Minnesota Vikings vs. Washington Redskins, Nov. 3, 1968; Dennis Morgan, Dallas Cowboys vs. St. Louis Cardinals, Oct. 13, 1974

Kickoff Return Records

Most Yardage Returning Kickoffs, Career—6,922, Ron Smith, Chicago Bears, Atlanta Falcons, Los Angeles Rams, San Diego Chargers, Oakland Raiders, 1965–1974

Most Yardage Returning Kickoffs, Season—1,345, Buster Rhymes, Minnesota Vikings, 1985

Most Yardage Returning Kickoffs, Game—294, Wally Triplett, Detroit Lions vs. Los Angeles Rams, Oct. 29, 1950

Longest Kickoff Return—106 yards, Al Carmichael, Green Bay Packers vs. Chicago Bears, Oct. 7, 1956; Noland Smith, Kansas City Chiefs vs. Denver Broncos, Dec. 17, 1967; Roy Green, St. Louis Cardinals vs. Dallas Cowboys, Oct. 21, 1979

Fumbles

Most Fumbles, Career—105, Roman Gabriel, Los Angeles Rams, 1962–1972; Philadelphia Eagles, 1973–1977

Most Fumbles, Season—17, Dan Pastorini, Houston Oilers, 1973; Warren Moon, Houston Oilers, 1984

Most Fumbles, Game—7, Len Dawson, Kansas City Chiefs vs. San Diego Chargers, Nov. 15, 1964

Miscellaneous Records

Most Seasons, Active Player—26, George Blanda, Chicago Bears, Baltimore Colts, Houston Oilers, Oakland Raiders, 1949–1975

Most Games Played, Career—340, George Blanda, Chicago Bears, Baltimore Colts, Houston Oilers, Oakland Raiders, 1949–1975

Super Bowl Records

Most Points, Career—24, Franco Harris, Pittsburgh Steelers

Most Points, Game—18, Roger Craig, San Francisco 49ers vs. Miami Dolphins, 1985

Most Touchdowns, Career—4, Franco Harris, Pittsburgh Steelers

Most Touchdowns, Game—3, Roger Craig, San Francisco 49ers vs. Miami Dolphins, 1985

Most Field Goals, Career—5, Ray Wersching, San Francisco 49ers

Most Field Goals, Game—4, Don Chandler, Green Bay Packers vs. Oakland Raiders, 1968; Ray Wersching, San Francisco 49ers vs. Cincinnati Bengals, 1982

Most Yards Gained, Career—354, Franco Harris, Pittsburgh Steelers

Most Yards Gained, Game—191, Marcus Allen, Los Angeles Raiders vs. Washington Redskins, 1984

Longest Run from Scrimmage—74 yards, Marcus Allen, Los Angeles Raiders vs. Washington Redskins, 1984

INDEX